THE ARCHAEOLOGY
OF NEGATIVE SPACE

THE ARCHAEOLOGY
OF NEGATIVE SPACE

Poems

Janet Wildung

FCP

Full Court Press
Englewood Cliffs, New Jersey

Published in the United States of America
by Full Court Press, 601 Palisade Avenue,
Englewood Cliffs, NJ 07632
fullcourtpress.com

ISBN 978-1-953728-06-7
Library of Congress Control No. 2022907164

Book design by Barry Sheinkopf

*Robert Lavett Smith has graciously allowed
the author to visit his town Calamity.*

To Mike

without whom my adult life
would have been far less fun
and my adult self thirty years lonelier

Acknowledgments

My heartfelt thanks to Bob Smith, whose support has been rock-solid and constant, and whose worth as a poetical sounding board for me is immeasurable.

My gratitude also to Vicki Van Ausdall for her willingness to apply her excellent editorial talents multiple times as my manuscript evolved from initial draft to galley proofs.

Note: No poets or editors were harmed in the making of this book.

Table of Contents

"I'm lookin' at ghosts and empties."
—*Paul Simon*

FADING TO BLACK

Grief: all tones of bitter white,
impotently raging with lack and longing;
the sky on a sunless day;
hospital sheets; chiseled granite.

Melancholy: a deep, golden gray
that glows, moody and languorous;
distant woodsmoke pierced
by late autumn sunlight.

Comfort: the darkest black;
the night fog enfolding this island
in its thick blanket that smells of salt
and ocean and bedrock, grit and survival.

THE EVENTUAL RAIN

Consider the fairy shrimp,
whose eggs might blow for fifty years
across the Arizona desert, waiting
for enough water to grow
and to mate.

How like love, then,
the eventual rain must seem, transforming
stones and soil into a sea of brilliant flowers;
sudden and brief,
but essential.

C IS FOR MOON

Candescent hammock
welcoming slumberous stars;
the crease of a smile;

a church bell's rhythm;
worn rim of a beggar's cup;
half a proffered coin;

a cradling arm;
the curl of a sleep-furled fist;
an eyelid's fringed curve;

the cadence of tides;
thirty seconds on the clock;
the course of a dream.

REACHING FOR THE BOTTOM

I woke today thinking about the lake
behind my grandmother's bungalow
where we spent time every summer
when I was a kid.

Barefoot, we'd step squarely
on the worn boards of the dock to avoid splinters,
although by the time it was late enough
in the season to swim, our soles were summer-tough.
Then we'd jump in to play: splashing; threading
the surface with our strong bodies; lazing
in faded black inner tubes, the rubber hot and pliant.

I'm back there, amid the weathered scents
of sun-baked wood; the shallows' dank, vegetable reek;
the papery shuffling click of dragonflies flashing
among the cattails; myriad water lilies crouched
on their leathery pads, stamped on the lake's murky hem.

I float suspended, arms gathering and releasing
the water, legs hanging down, swaying in the gentle jostle.

My head is warm in the grace of the sun,
but the velvety silt at my feet chills me, and unseen
plants slide around my ankles, languid and dangerous.
As always, I can't bring myself to go deeper, far enough
to reach the bottom.

I've never been able to determine
whether I'm afraid to touch the unknown
solidity of the lake bed, or I'm afraid I never will,
sinking, then pulled unchecked
into cold, inky depths.

BLOOD AND CREAM

Summer swims in the lake
always meant two things:

Sitting on the dock
for a few minutes, scraping
dark, bloated leeches
from our bodies, their round marks
bloody on our wet skin.

Strolling back from the pavilion
with fresh peach ice cream,
our mouths attached
to that sweetness, sucking
and licking the dripping cones.

NO FISHING TONIGHT

A rough sea splatters
the milky moonlight; if they
want to drink, let them.

A MATTER OF COURSE

If I place my hands on my shoulders,
I can feel them: small nubs
beneath the skin. They grow
larger each night.

Some morning I know
I'll wake with wings lifting me
higher and higher until I'm a tiny speck,
a bright balloon that won its freedom
from a careless hand.

ON MY HARSH MISTRESS

Insomnia's a wicked one: no sleep
permitted while I diligently write,
attempting to engender something deep
and marvelously new before the night
with all its lucent beauty seeps away.
It's then the muse restores herself, while I
surrender to the stupor of the day,
at work and uninspired, red of eye.
Nocturnal nonetheless, I ply my art
this time to spin a sonnet up, and so
I desperately strive to voice my heart
and thoughts in formal verse—but I just know:
If I myself had world enough and time,
I'd get this goddamned poem to *soar* in rhyme.

NEIGHBORHOOD BIRDS

Rock Pigeons

Urgently crooning,
coaxing the sun's voice to knife
through the blunting fog.

Alameda Song Sparrows

Knots of brown ribbon
shifting in morning's soft cloth,
fluttering the air.

Anna's Hummingbirds

Pirouetting blurs
of tulle, faces graciously
pressed into bouquets.

Common Ravens

Dark punctuation
in the naked sycamore's
illegible scrawl.

California Gulls

Laughter sailing high
in the afternoon, foam blown
from the wind-struck bay.

Steller's Jays　　　　　Flashing in the yard,
　　　　　　　　　　　scattered shards of fallen blue
　　　　　　　　　　　limned by city soot.

Mourning Doves　　　　Insistent as rain,
　　　　　　　　　　　sighing, questioning, aching
　　　　　　　　　　　through the dying light.

Marbled Godwits　　　　Startled, thundering
　　　　　　　　　　　into the deepening sky,
　　　　　　　　　　　igniting the stars.

Great Horned Owls　　　Executioners
　　　　　　　　　　　working the scaffolds of night,
　　　　　　　　　　　swift and terrible.

REFLECTIONS: METAL ON METAL

Trains groan their big jazz chords,
yearning to slip the forced monotony
of the rails, to know instead, say,
the lightness, the exhilaration a bullet feels
as the hard shove of exploding powder sends it
arcing, flying free toward an unknown future.

Bullets dream of becoming trains.

SOJOURN

For Scott

We have gone then, you and I,
and gotten drunk across the bay
for the hell of it one fine afternoon.

After the twilight ferry back
from Larkspur, we find we have to pee,
and so we make a beeline for the pay toilet
at the foot of Market. You fumble
into a pocket to get us each a quarter, but instead
yank out a fistful of loose change that bursts
from your hand, scattering sudden stars
on the dusky cobbled sky around your feet,
ringing like laughter, bright as applause.

When we're done, we part ways, leaving
those transient constellations where they lie,
navigating home by instinct alone.

POETRY LUNCH

Limericks make for a fine appetizer,
and haikus a light, restrained dessert.

What to eat between, though?

Sestinas seem overly fussy, but
blank verse can be very tasty if seasoned properly.
Villanelles should be avoided: they repeat.
Sonnets must be washed, cooked thoroughly,
and accompanied by wine, preferably vintage.
Odes, on the other hand, are best served raw,
sans garnish.

Decisions, decisions. . . .

JAILBREAK

Sudden wings
flicker the bars of sunlight
that hold me in my chair.
My heart follows
their shadows.

LATE ON
A SUNLESS AFTERNOON

Birds cross overhead,
a secular blessing sketched
on billowed white robes.

IRON, BOUND

For reasons of his own,
my father wrapped a horseshoe
around the trunk of our blue spruce,
then just a sapling.

Over the years,
the wood slowly embraced
the metal until not even a scar
betrayed its presence.

But I remember:
Beneath the dust-blue indecision,
deep in the yielding fiber
resides a core of iron.

SUPERMARKET INTRIGUE

Armies of soup in their smart uniforms,
herds of dumb, obedient cereal,
frozen foods—
it's all so stacked, so orderly, so
predictable.

Over in produce, however,
things are much more unruly:
Onions shift, uneasy in their papery skins;
carrots sprawl wantonly while celery stalks,
pale and rigid, look on in disapproval,
and beets darken further with lust;
ears of corn grin slyly
behind their green silk scarves; quietly,
upstart mushrooms foment rebellion.

JUST ANOTHER
SAN FRANCISCO MORNING

I sit on the beach,
wrapped in a cream-colored blanket,
drinking coffee.

It's one of those ethereal mornings
when it's impossible to discern
where ocean ends and sky begins,
so I can easily believe that the water and the air
and the sand and the blanket and I
are the same matter,
matter the same.

Later, bittersweet sun
will leak through the fog,
reimposing boundaries.

RESOLUTIONS

I will
tease fire from your mouth,
inhale you until you are froth
in my blood, drink you deep.

I will
lay claim to your wilds:
survey, mark, and map you,
make your canyons howl and echo,
quench your deserts.

I will
give the ache in you wings,
make you float like gravity isn't
your other constant
lover.

I will.

I will.

DISCOVERY

You're the opposite
of a geode: all dull rock
inside; nothing more.

A HOLE IN THE SIDEWALK RESEMBLES PERU

The hole is an old one,
the slabs of the surrounding sidewalk
buckled and broken years ago by trees
flexing their questing roots.

Down in the exposed earth, a colony
of ants has built a citadel, step by step,
over the course of one golden summer.

In late September, an imperious
sycamore leaf, pushed by a stiff wind, sails across
the sidewalk and invades, a sudden scourge
on the civilization and its works.

The ants resist, fighting fiercely,
but the leaf is heavy and destructive, and the ants
finally flee their fallen home for new grounds.

Over time, the leaf disintegrates
into bronze flecks that slowly darken to dust,
its ruins indistinguishable from dirt.

DRY

One August day
in my teens, I stood
in my New Jersey backyard
reveling in the pouring rain,
utterly drenched.

Here in California,
summer is relentlessly sunny.

Oh, to be completely wet
again, standing in the soft grass,
soft and wet on my naked feet,
face upturned to the weeping sky
feeling the rain run off me in sheets,
soaking wet, fully soaked, fully
alive, open, ready for all invasions,
all assaults, all storms.

EVOCATION

After the starkness of memory's landscape,
shadowy craters awash in dark dust,
birds paint the morning with full-throated color,
licking the glorious canvas of dawn.

SEVEN TITLES FOR A NONEXISTENT SERIES OF CHILDREN'S BOOKS

1. *Minaret Soufflé and the Roadkill Tissue Box*
2. *Minaret Soufflé and the Malodorous Duck*
3. *Minaret Soufflé and the Tiny Couch*
4. *Minaret Soufflé and the Earwax Mausoleum*
5. *Minaret Soufflé and the Recalcitrant Spoon*
6. *Minaret Soufflé and the Noodling Boils*
7. *Minaret Soufflé Rides the Bus*

TRANSIT

The November fog dampens
everything: the exhausted grind
of the 48-Quintara as it lurches westward
past the bleak pastels of endless row houses;
the smells of wet wool, sweat, noodles,
and jasmine tea that fill the chilly interior;
the muffled rustle of plastic grocery bags
slackened by age and use; the flat drone
of stop announcements no one needs to hear.
Even the fluorescent light fails, just a yawn
dying into the uniformly dark clothing
worn by all on board. Despite the constant jostle,
respectful distances are maintained.

Out of nowhere,
a sudden squall of girls gusts
onto the bus, fresh from the school day,
a turbulent whirl of color and sound—
all limbs, hair, bangles, backpacks, cell phones—
the very air crackles around them
in happy chattering chaos. And then

just as startlingly, they're off,
blowing down the avenues, the vibrant confetti
of their voices tumbling, floating down
to the wet pavement.

With a studied care something like relief,
the remaining passengers sigh, shift, and settle
further into the seats, aging frames still remembering
their distant spring, while the bus carries them on
haltingly but surely toward the Sunset.

GREEN TEA

For Robert Lavett Smith

Each and every morning,
I swallow cold tea like a benediction:
a luminous hint of darkness just past,
a weapon which alone can defend
against the assault of the coming day
that rips me from sleep's welcome oblivion.
It soothes and cools my heated throat
like the multitudinous blessing of rain,
ever allowing me to forgive
how the dawn seemingly slaughters
a tenuous peace that's really
always there, how the sweetness
that lingers on my tongue
presages the night ahead.

THE SLOW DANCE
OF TURNING STARS

Some nights, it seems
I could so easily walk for miles
in the shimmering dark, seeking
a rhythm greater than my own breathing,
in time with the slow dance
of turning stars.

In the end, I too will dance
and burn, my body the smoke
that mingles with the cold air,
my soul the heat
that always
rises.

DAILY SERVICE

The night spreads its shroud
on the bare and broken bones
of the fallen day.

FJORD: ONE PHOTO, FOUR TAKES

In love (requited): One lover's knees spread wide,
welcoming home the other.

In love (unrequited): Empty vee, aching to be filled
with more than just the air, the blue.

In mourning: Plundered earth,
a furrow cut hard, still bleeding ice water.

On vacation: Great view.

A POETRY TUTORIAL

The Basics

1. Raw Material
    Lay out your thoughts longhand;
    say all you want to say, and more, even;
    scrawl beyond the borders, top the brim—
    just make sure you have enough.

2. Scope
    Pare without mercy;
    remove what doesn't belong
    until you have a carving
    that feels true in your hand.

3. Design
    Turn and fold;
    smooth line over line
    until you have a crane
    worthy of the other 999.

4. Construction
    Crumple the words;
    crush them down on themselves

until you have a diamond,
dense and flashing, with edges that cut.

5. Quality Check
Read aloud: Taste each word; feel
how your mouth and tongue dance together
to form each syllable; adjust the fit
until you have music.

6. Final Acceptance
a. Repeat steps 1 through 5 as needed.
b. Have someone else read it.
c. Apply one of the following finishes:
 • Repeat steps 6a and 6b as needed.
 • Release it into the world.
 • Scrap the whole thing and start over.

Advanced Techniques

1. Set aside what you learned about the basics.

2. Do what works.

FIRE EXTINGUISHER

For JS

You ignited me
one April evening
with your flame blue eyes,
your smoky mouth.

And so we burned together
for a while. It amused me that you used the top
of a vintage brass fire extinguisher
as an ashtray. Sharing a few English Ovals,
you once taught me how to blow a perfect ring.
Near the end of it all, you swore, voice blazing
so earnestly, you'd walk through fire for me.

By then, I'd known
that didn't include *my* fire.
And yet, when you finally left me
the part of me that was yours
still died hard
into ash.

THE SORROW OF HENS

Every day, she mourns
her future, taken piece
by piece so casually. O void,
where once was such promise!

Every night, she dreams
of yellow: a sunlit yard, life
in happy tumult
around her.

PINK PEARL

Ah, Pink Pearl: ubiquitous denizen
of artists' lofts and sketchers' kits;
item on every list of drawing materials
required for class on day one;

distant and far more splendid cousin
to those lowly, metal-bound nubs
abiding with pencils in quiet servitude
to accountants and the like.

Behold the innocence, the pale purity
of an unused Pearl, unsullied
by the casual corruption of life,
the grimy residue from others' waywardness.

You beveled beauty!
Solid, dependable, ever flexible—
do you feel the grit of the pumice within you,
an ancestral tug from your fiery origins?

You coax unwanted graphite
from where it has strayed, embracing it
even as you lose parts of yourself
to the rough caress of the page.

How I wish I could so simply
employ you to erase my errant history,
to urge my blurred self
back to the sharpness of my youth.

SUMMER 2020

Darkened orange sky,
somber light low as a moan.
California burns.

HERE, JOY IS BLUE

A rectangle of exuberant sky
I captured, shot straight up
one clear afternoon during the summer wildfires,
so whenever the winds shift again
and the days rise acrid and dim,
a fragment of joy still exists
where I can find it.

AUTUMN IN NEW YORK WITH EUBIE BLAKE

Late February, 2022

> "Be grateful for luck.
> Pay the thunder no mind—listen to the birds.
> And don't hate nobody."
> —*Eubie Blake*

I'm having dinner
with Eubie, sharing noodle soup
made by his caregiver.
Despite the glare and chaos outside,
the room is dim and peaceful,
and the soup delicious.

Ella and Satch are singing
"Autumn in New York," their voices supple
and rich, meandering
through golden melancholy,
urban and urbane, and indeed
so inviting.

Eubie's face fractures gently
into innumerable wrinkles as he smiles

and nods, head cocked,
long brown fingers ghosting
over the table, playing along.

I wake to hear a mourning dove
at my window.

NAVIGATION

For RC

Tonight I remember a sunny day,
the bay sharp with sailboats, and I feel again
as I did that more distant night: my hands on
your hard, bared thighs; my heart laid open
by the blade of your smile.

Decades have passed,
but part of me is still lost, still amazed
that the same wind that hauls the breath
from my lungs also moves ships
across a vast and seamless sea.

Lacking a sextant,
mapless, stars doused by fog,
I try my hand at navigation
using only a creased photograph and a sweater
that smells of your tobacco.

I lay out these lines, tenuous
tracings the requisite chart;

I craft this vessel, transparent as glass to all,
but its true message, like a whisper
placed in the shell of your ear,
will make landfall only
if it ever reaches you.

THE HEART AT LOW TIDE

Spent chambers shiver,
guarded yet fiercely yearning
for a new moon's pull.

IRON UNBOUND

Even iron moves:
stretching and clenching
as the temperature shifts;
blossoming slowly into rust
wherever moisture has touched it;
trembling when every atom within
realigns in helpless response
to a magnet's lure.

Think of this
the next time you feel caged,
bars drawn tight across your heart.

JANET WILDUNG

THE GEESE ANNOUNCE
THEY'RE LEAVING

Exultant brushstrokes,
a dark victory sign swept
across a pale page.

NATURE SCHOOLS US, TWICE

Before going to bed, we put the scant remains
of our dinner in the empty garbage can outside.
Late the next morning, we discover
that we hadn't closed the can lid tightly, and now
the discarded takeout boxes contain
an apocalyptic number of maggots, wriggling
vigorously in heaped clumps.

Horrified, we hose out the can, casting
the whole mess over the driveway, hoping
that the combination of black tarmac and summer sun
will dry the creatures out and prevent a plague of flies.
Glancing out the window a short time later, however,
we watch as a flock of small birds
rapidly carpets it all
and consumes the feast.

NIGHT AND DAY

1.

Night glances at the clock and sighs.
Day is late. Again.

Day finally arrives, loud and bold as brass.
Night grimaces, exasperated.

Day is unrepentant, whistling jauntily.
Night glares.

Night hands Day another dead soldier.
Day opens the blinds.

Night gives Day the latest manuscript.
Day tears it up.

Night leaves a mess.
Day tries to clean up but, as is often the case, falls short.

...

Night quietly settles in to watch the evening news.
Day puts the last of the dishes away.

Night is tired of always having to take the trash out.
Day laughs.

Day hands Night a cup of tea.
Night turns on the lights.

Day goes down the front steps two at a time.
Night falls softly onto a chaise and sips the tea. For now.

Day leaves a mess.
Night cleans up, grousing *sotto voce*.

2.

Day shines.
Night reflects.

Day demands.
Night persuades.

Day consumes.
Night replenishes.

Day tenses.
Night releases.

Day struts, graceless, borders on boorish.
Night glides, flows, stretches languorously.

Night thrusts.
Day parries.

Day screws around.
Night gets shit done.

Night keeps score.
Day keeps score, secretly.

Night unearths.
Day buries.

Night nitpicks, mulls, and often regrets.
Day acts and copes—at least, ostensibly.

Night from time to time despairs.
Day never does.

3.

Night is sometimes harsh, sometimes just plain aloof.
Day is sometimes harsh, sometimes just plain indifferent.

Day can be a real bastard but knows how to get away with it.
Night can be a real bastard but knows how to get away with it.

LATER THAN MIDNIGHT

The new decade is barely twenty minutes old.
In the distance, the steady rumble and drumskin
splatters of fireworks persist, while
something with claws scrabbles ferociously
outside my bedroom window: a vicious sound,
a dead-of-night sound, sharp against the low rolling
explosions bludgeoning the darkness. The new decade is barely
twenty minutes old, and already it sounds
like the end of days.

A QUESTION OF PERSPECTIVE

"I still do," he murmured. "I never stopped."

I looked at him across the table as he slowly, delicately, shredded his napkin, eyes downcast. And just like that, it was as if layers of the past had been shed. Okay, not quite just like that, but it served to focus us. I watched his hands as he balled up the napkin tatters. If I held my fork up in front of my eye, I could put him behind bars, as it were, trapping him in this moment, stopping time. Or perhaps I was already the one imprisoned.

And the ancient sun hung low in the sky, bronzing everything forever.

ANOTHER MATTER, OF COURSE

Some days
it's all I can do
to keep from pulling
my own wings off.

A LIFE IN POETRY

You're reminded repeatedly
"First the stairs"—like that's a surprise?
Like you'll *forget??*
It's a fifth-floor walk-up, fer crissakes:
Stairs are always first, coming or going. Duh.

You wonder at peaches, ya-honk at the geese,
live in places lit only by glasses of milk
(which leads to some interesting sartorial results,
though you admit it saves big-time on electricity);
and you constantly, shamelessly raid other people's refrigerators:
The food just tastes better that way, you tell yourself;
you don't always leave a note.

When you wander, you're lonely, and the damned daffodils
can only do so much. You're terrible with directions,
often getting lost on less traveled roads
you should *never* have taken. When you go down
to the sea, despite what you ask, you know you need more
than a tall ship, a star, blah, blah, blah
(I mean, what about food and *drink,* for starters?!), so. . .yeah.
More.

You play strip poker with the best minds of your generation,
giggling hysterically every time you say you'll see them
before raising, and their tells are so obvious
that you always smirk to yourself, "beat" in*deed.*
One of your oldest friends has black teeth,
but you love the rude bastard anyway, you really do,
because he tells it like it is. And that new preacher—
Basalt? eh, something like that—*he's* a live one all right.

You recollect emotion only in tranquility;
some lovers complain but most don't. In fact,
you've been told that during sex, your mouth
makes some pretty impressive desolate zeros
and you're considerate enough to prove *all* your pleasures.
Also, as it turns out, you end with a bang
and a whimper. Who knew?

And what is *with* all the toads? Seriously.

All kidding aside, though, there's one thing you know
more surely than anything else you've ever known:
Wisdom comes from the darkness
and we call it poetry. It is still pain.

OISEAUX

Today again, the birds
are speaking French.

One urges *vite, vite*
as if I weren't already
aware of time whipping me
harder as the years go by.

One intones *bijou*
repeatedly, wielding it
like an auditory talisman;
glowing, it frequents my dreams.

We age, fear grows—
true in any language.

AUGUST 1918

i.m. Lilie Govers Wildung (1899–2000)

My grandmother is perched saucily
in a tree, laughing down at the photographer.
Her dark wavy hair clasped by a headband,
legs crossed at the ankle, long white dress ablaze
even in the shade of the glowing leaves,
she is the essence of summer.
It's in black-and-white, of course,
but her exuberance, her vitality
makes the colors sing out anyway.
You see the fresh green of those leaves,
the living heat in her face as surely
as if the moment were captured on Kodachrome.

When I first saw her so long ago,
so alive, I was astonished:
The woman I'd grown up knowing
bore no traces of that day or anything like it.
But her husband, fun-loving and warm,
had lit that shaded girl like the sun,
and when he died one Valentine's Day,
well before old age, he left her there
in winter, shuttered permanently;
summer never touched her eyes again.

DARK ON DARK

"as if sandpaper could sing"
—*Joyce Carol Oates (on Bob Dylan)*

More aware than the oblivious pigeons
meandering through the streets for easy crumbs,
ravens are the folk singers
who redefine and call out the world
in their own rough voices.

More moving than the querulous mourning doves
carrying on about heaven knows what,
ravens are the blues singers
who recognize Death at a distance
and croon to soothe it in its lonely mission.

More knowing than the vacuous flycatchers
tweeting hysterically at the everyday dawn,
ravens are the prophets
who urgently mutter their warnings,
naming madness and destruction to come.

More honest than the saccharine nightingales
whose liquid lies promise impossible beauty,
ravens are the poets
who lay truth bare; the naked ink
with which darkness is written
so all can see.

A SMALL COLLECTION
OF HOME MOVIES

For Joe

Reel 1 (snippet): Durham

Me reading you my latest poems;
you telling me once
that as you hitched from New Hampshire
to New Jersey in freezing rain,
only the steady jab of your backpack
at your hips confirmed you were still alive
and not facedown in a ditch alongside I-95 South;
and that as you walked, you thought of home,
calling it vague and indifferent;
me writing a poem about *that*
and reading it to you.

Reel 2: Dover

A poster of Gérôme's *Pygmalion and Galatea*,
paled to blues by years of light
through the narrow bathroom window.
The tiny kitchen, forever imbued with the smells
of scorched tomato sauce, dish soap,

and that sweet-musty essence of old house.
Languorous evenings in the dim cavern
of the living room, lit by a single streetlamp
and occasional moonlight;
sprawled in darkness, wrapped in music,
we speak of everything and nothing.
In the attic bedroom, with its deep dormers,
ancient wallpaper in a yellow and brown foulard print,
the white door you've been using as a writing desk,
you and your guitar do your best Neil Young
as I lounge on a bare mattress, gazing up at the art
postcards pinned to the slanted ceiling.
Back stairs draped in their morning fabrics of sun and pine,
deftly quilted by the staccato stitching
of a nearby woodpecker.

Reel 3 (snippet): Union

The Traveler Restaurant, our usual stop for lunch,
coffee, pie, and, of course, books. I find a first edition
of Burgess's *Animal Stories*; you, some Updike.

Reel 4 (snippet): Westport

Following the sinuous road through the woods,
I'm having trouble staying awake. Coffee
at The Three Bears Restaurant, then we're back in the car.

Reel 5: Highlands

Lazy summer afternoon
in one of the beachside cabins out back,
tasting the salt and rotting kelp on the breeze,
discussing your manuscript while I silently admire
your strong runner's legs and elegant hands.
That evening, hot and crowded close
in a bar, a sparkling kaleidoscope
of laughter, glass, and booze shot through
with an insistent "Crossroads" groove,
live and electric.
We're up the rest of the night drinking
vodka and peach schnapps with one of your brothers,
sitting at a long table in the basement
of your parents' boardinghouse.
Come the hazy bloodred dawn,
I manage to make it outside alone
to the beach, sit, dig a hole, vomit,
smooth the sand back into place;
and I drift there, my back to the house, resolutely
avoiding the water, sure that if I give in
to my desire for its cool embrace,
it'll pull me under and I'll drown.
Some time later, you find me
and take me inside to the green room

with the vintage dresser,
and I sleep.

Reel 6 (snippet): Jersey City

On our way to the Met
trying to catch the next city-bound bus,
you crossing tracks just ahead of a train,
me
hesitating
a moment too long, and we're separated,
dark engine bearing down just yards away,
coming at us like the future.

THE YEARS AND WE
ARE WRIT IN FIRE

1.

The promise sprouts urgently
in livid green: at the swollen tips
of waking trees ignited by the scratch
of a mackerel sky; flaring between
the broad planks of earth in furrowed fields
where seedlings unfold and blind bulbs push
their tongues up to taste the morning sun.
Lovers trail sparks through the blankets
of dusk; the yearning calls of spring peepers
throb all night until dawn.

2.

Flames beat in our blood and we are ablaze,
roaring, resplendent; consuming and consumed.
Fat flowers burn everywhere;
the edges of the day are scorched
by the pressure-cooker rasp of cicadas;

and fitful lightning cracks the rain down
to sizzle on the grateful pavement.
As heat yields to the charry night,
fireflies dance, fragmented echoes
of the spent sunlight, the hot stars.

3.

Bright embers drift from their lofty hearths,
cooling as they fall through the smoky breath
of late afternoon, crackling underfoot.
Fleeting as spattered soot, geese fly
under blue clouds licked by beaten gold.
We take our slowing selves inside
to escape the deepening chill,
glowing until twilight singes us
and we give in to the darkness, lulled
by the crickets' flickering chirr.

4.

Sketched in charcoal, buildings dwindle
upward into blankness, delicately rendered
in muted hues of stone, slate, asphalt, ice.
A pitch wind slips through the dreaming streets,

tagging the bark of trunks imprisoned
in iron grates and dead leaves dazzled with frost.
Cremated or buried, we all become still
as breathless ash; then we're gone,
claimed by the dirt, the sea, the air,
beyond even the memory of fire.

CIVIL TWILIGHT

As my neighbor scours his garbage bins,
the water's whispered howl roughs the stillness
of this breathless June evening.

Not far distant,
persistent sirens beckon
necessary unrest,
the order of the day
in this town.

This state.

This world.

MORNING GLORIES

i.m. Elisabeth (Elsa) Reiber Lampe (1907–1970)

Before she had her garden in the suburbs,
my grandmother strung lattices of cotton twine
over the window of their Bronx apartment
for morning glories to climb.
There they would fiercely cling,
their gentle, astonished faces like living mirrors,
yellow smudges nestled in centers
of wide open blue.

She'd found a way to speak without vocal cords,
severed in goiter surgery years before I was born.
I found her ruined voice soothing, like purring,
whenever she read to me,
my favorite story one about a mouse
who lived in a guitar and learned to make music,
plucking the strings softly at night.

Sitting on her kitchen floor,
I'd play with her crystal necklace,
turning it in the sunlight, watching the colors wheel

and dance around the room; at the table, she and my mother
would visit over coffee and homemade *Butterkuchen*,
the coarse sugar surface flashing
its own tiny, sweet prisms.

BREATHS TAKEN, BREATHS RELEASED

i.m. Fritz Arthur Emil Lampe (1906–1970)

Soot from the Bronx streets
inevitably permeated everything inside; so
once a year, he cleaned all of the household clocks
to ensure their inner workings remained in good order.
He protected the kitchen table
with newspapers and opened the housings one by one;
using a small paintbrush, different for each
according to size, he patiently swept every gear,
every delicate movement with carbon tetrachloride,
then laid them out to dry. And over time,
as he worked, the vapors plumed invisibly,
stealing into his lungs to pervade blood and tissue,
blowing life into the sparks of nascent cancer
that eventually settled in his bones
like molten tar.

These days, in my house near San Francisco,
I keep wool sweaters and cedar sachets
in the little brown linen cabinet he built from scrap lumber
shortly after he married my grandmother.

His talented hands planed and shaped the humble wood,
creating a sturdy, capable piece
with an elegant edge and a bright nickel latch.
In humid weather, the whispered scent
of his cigarette smoke always makes me smile as I walk past,
the glossy finish still holding his breath, still breathing out
fifty years after his death.

SMALL LUXURIES

One of thirteen children,
my grandfather grew up in Berlin
in crushing poverty; his father had died early
from tuberculosis, leaving the rest of the family
to do what they could to survive.

Mostly, they ate whatever
discarded vegetables they could find
in the alleys behind the grocers.

But some days, his mother went at dawn
to the neighborhood bakeries, who allowed her to scrape
their used pans to gather crumbs; from these and water,
she would make a small cake.

And once, one of his brothers
brought home an unexpected find.
They ate their meal slowly that day, savoring
the rare luxury of roasted meat. When asked
what kind it was, his brother said *miau* and grinned;
after the briefest of pauses,
they continued eating.

TRANSITORY RICHES

The notes of Chopin nocturnes
drop like pearls, flaring
briefly against the velvet night.

GEORGE AND THE LONG GREEN

i.m. George Henry Wildung, Jr. (1931–2015)

Dad's job in corporate finance didn't afford him
the opportunity to cultivate the green
he really cared about. And so he grew vegetables
in a narrow strip of ground along one side
of our backyard. That garden, though tiny
by farm standards, was lush and magnificent
each year from high summer well into autumn.

There were cucumbers, grounded zeppelins festooned
with a rococo riot of curlicues; dark, glossy eggplants
filling slowly like balloons under star-shaped nozzles;
feathery fronds belying the placid solidity of carrots hidden
below them; the beautiful geometry of Brussels sprouts
spiraling tightly along their stalks.

We'd stand there, hip deep in living produce, grazing:
perfectly ripe Jersey tomatoes hot from the vine,
seeds and juice dripping over our chins and hands;
thick-lobed sweet peppers; green beans, slender
and crisp; a scallion here, a lettuce leaf there.

He insisted we pick ripe corn only when
the pot was near boiling so the shucked ears
could be slipped into the water mere minutes after harvest;
all sugars thus preserved, those kernels popped
and crunched in our mouths, sweet as peacetime.

Helping reap a crop of horseradish late one October
had me straining with all my might to dislodge
an especially stubborn specimen, imagining all the while
that the bastard had to go a yard deep. When the root finally
yielded, I beheld with wonder and consternation
a squat cone about three inches long.

I can still see him, carefully tending
the flats of seedlings he raised under grow lights
in the safety of the garage, making sure
they were ready to survive before he moved them
outside into the world.

NIGHT TAKES SAN FRANCISCO

"Quand San Francisco s'embrume,
Quand San Francisco s'allume,
San Francisco. . .
Où êtes-vous ?"
　　　—Maxime Le Forestier

Beyond here lies the restless Pacific,
stuttering on the jagged shoreline, caught
between the rocks and the gleaming blade
of the horizon sharp in the lambent haze.

The last breaths of dying sunlight warm
the advancing fog, huge blue billows
that crest the hills above the shattered bay
and roll like silent thunder down
into the shadowed valleys.

As night prowls westward, sparks spread
through the darkening land, fleeting
shows of defiance doomed to fail:
The black ocean rises into the black night,
into the blackened fog, and the city swoons
into all that darkness; and settles; and sleeps late,
reluctant to face the morning's judgment.

BIRTHDAY

It isn't wind that stirs the air to flight,
but passing time, its touch like subtle steel
upon my neck. The unrelenting light
makes shadows glare, and I could even feel,
despite the sky's cerulean expanse,
this breath of summer heat in early May
is actually eager death that pants,
pursuing me and gaining every day.
Not Thompson's hound of heaven, though, for sure:
no god or rabid dogma drawing near;
religion's a placebo, not a cure.
Most likely, there's just space beyond this sphere:
a patient darkness lurking out of view;
the ever present black behind the blue.

NEW YEAR

The wet road glows, lit
by the silver sky of dawn,
shining like a knife.

LES BARICADES MISTÉRIEUSES

Söllscher's version spreads
across my restless mind: a moiré pattern
of plush rain shivering the surface
of a midnight lake; silken threads
of sound burnished further each time
they smooth over me; a luminous shield
against the merciless darkness—
and there is nowhere in those shadows
music doesn't reach, at least for a while.

WHAT I KNOW

I never have nightmares, I tell a friend,
and it's true: I don't.

Here's something else that's true:
Sometimes I wake, my throat strained and rough,
the air thrown flat to the walls for an instant,
the echo of an echo trembling in my ears;
like the stinging imprint of a slap I didn't feel;
like the elusive light in my head that seeps
from the corner of my right eye, that I can't ever
turn fast enough to really see.

MEASURED BY THE YARD

"What does your yard say about you?"
an unsolicited email challenges.

All sorts of things, I imagine.

Sharp-tongued grass spikes
rumors through its sparse community
like wildfire; last year's fallen leaves
provide ample fodder for gossipy weeds,
while dead bushes stand
in silent judgment; even normally reticent
earthworms dish the dirt.
Trash blown here from other yards
loiters insolently, daring me
to step outside and do something about it.

What does it say about me?

Perhaps simply that I've been too busy
dealing with interior issues
to worry much about anything else.

I let it go.

SOMETIMES I DREAM
WE ARE WHOLE AGAIN

and not simply fragments
struggling to distinguish ourselves
from the ruins our lives have become,
our flesh weak, and whatever spirit remains
willing and able only to write.

This is now the marriage of our true minds,
the sole partner left on our dance cards,
and so we dance.

It is enough, you say
in response to my question,
even if this does turn out to be true.
It is enough, you avow
in writing.

Well.

It had better be.

It *must* be.

It will be until it isn't,
until you and I
aren't.

THE BONES WITHIN

A flashlight's beam
through my fingers reveals
blood vessels, dusky traceries
on radiant ruby windows,
but the bones within
remain inviolate, stubbornly
resisting capture by so crude
an invasion.

ICE IN LEMONADE

As evening lingers, light
from the falling sun tints everything
a bleak yellow, more December
than July, a reminder that even now
days are on the wane:
Early summer's open hand, warm
and guileless, has already begun to tighten
into its winter fist, eventually
bruising the thin skies spread taut
over the shivering land.

THE PATCHWORK ME

Lying on my bed
in the softly decaying light
of a rainy afternoon,
I feel faded and fraying,
worn to near gossamer
wherever I've borne the most.

Pieced over time,
experience by experience,
the patchwork me has been quilted
by those who've touched me,
minute scars where each needle
pierced me still tangible,
still threaded with the pain or joy
that accompanied it.

The day disintegrates
into darkness, and someday
so will I, unraveled
by death's fine, sure hands.

AT THE LOST
AND PROFOUND

. . .the fingerprints of serial killers
the breath of stillborn children
the unwritten music of the newly dead
the dreams of amnesiacs
the whimpers of murdered futures
the tears of the damned. . .

Surely there's something of yours here, too.

DYING IN CHRYSALIS

For you, there will be
no moist wings unfolding,
that first dizzying drop
into the blaze of the day,
the air solidifying beneath you
as you push against it,
hungry, ecstatic.

This is all you'll get:
Your tender worm heart will be killed
by its own protective shield—
once a comfort, now a prison built too well—
struggling in its confines,
growing older and weaker
while you dream of flight
and your future dims to black.

You will fly instead as dust,
your brittle coffin cracked open at last
by a casual tread, swept up
with broken twigs and brown leaves
clenched like fists.

WHALE CARCASS ON OCEAN BEACH

The stench of rotting blubber,
even at a distance, is overwhelming,
the surrounding air oily and thick.
Although I leave after only a few moments,
it lingers on me and in me
for hours; on the beach,
saltwater rags scrub endlessly,
unable to cleanse the corrupted sand.

.

THIS YEAR

"Simply having a wonderful Christmastime."
—*Paul McCartney*

The first notes of "Jingle Bells"
sound to me this year like an alarm.
At 1:39 am on the 25th, a protracted argument
begins in the backyard next door, ensuring
no silent night. Even the moon's pallid light
is shrouded, and it's obvious that wise men
continue to be in acutely short supply.

For the first time in my 57 years,
I'm not under the same roof as my mother
on Christmas Day. Instead, we visit and
watch each other open presents
via a three-way video call with my brother
that takes us 20 minutes of fumbling
to get set up; despite multiple attempts
to center ourselves on our various devices,
parts of us remain cut off,
and we miss a lot.

We assure each other that we're lucky:
We're still together, albeit digitally.
But there's no mistaking a subtle shift,
the start of a widening distance that is surely
the specter of yuletides to come.

REMEMBERING GETTYSBURG

January 6, 2021

On an oppressively stormy day
in the summer of 1983,
I visited Gettysburg. I stood in a copse
along one side of the silent field,
feeling the weight
of the invisible dead still
there, warm rain darkening
the soil beneath them.

Today, in this increasingly bitter winter,
we all stand at the edge
of an even greater battlefield,
fractured by hate and bigotry,
familiar enemies even now
to which so many remain enslaved.

What more will it take
for us to resolve for good
to heed the better angels of our nature,
to honor all those who have died to preserve

this nation? Fail in this, and we
and our democracy shall indeed
perish from the earth.

THE MONKEYS SING MOZART

"Forgiveness is the fragrance that the violet sheds
on the heel that has crushed it."
—Mark Twain (attribution disputed)

After they finish Shakespeare,
the infinite monkeys tackle Mozart's Requiem.

Their Sanctus is jubilant,
lilting gracefully to its triumphal finish,
but it's their Lacrimosa
that really leaves an impression,
its plea piercingly beautiful, their eyes
wet and haunted.

DREAMING OF PETRICHOR

I am the ashes I scattered
a lifetime ago, heavy on the tense earth.

I am gutter dust that has forgotten
the taste of water, forgotten
there ever was such a thing as water.

I am smoke, the wind, a whisper.

And yet

sometimes I'm startled
by a faint thrill, like a favorite scent
from years ago that blows by me
on the street, and I'm unsure
whether it's real or just a memory
ambushing me, improbable as a raindrop
from a clear blue sky.

I look up anyway, searching
for the edge of a storm.

IRREDEEMABLE LOSSES

2020

Spring

Increased bigotry
and hate hold decency down,
gain a stranglehold,
whipped onward exultantly
by the presidential scourge.

Protesters, dispersed,
gather again and again,
dense clouds that promise
a hard rain but deliver
nothing like a watershed.

Widely scattered crops
of kindness and tolerance
prove meager indeed,
leave us empty, starved even
for basic civility.

Summer

Firefighters hang
tough, defying exhaustion,
the crackle and roar
of flames that deafen their ears,
destruction that fills their eyes.

Still, towns are gutted,
stinking ash and rubble wrapped
in a toxic haze,
sunlight dim and stained amber,
while the western U.S. burns.

In the desert, dead
Joshua trees stand aghast,
blackened and shrunken,
a mute shriek of branches raised
toward an unforgiving sky.

Autumn

The number of deaths
exceeds 300,000
as a virus wastes
the nation, spurred by rampant
and malignant indifference.

Hospitals strain, choked
by the relentless swell of
the desperately sick.
The ethical among us
keep faith in the greater good.

Deniers persist,
claiming their spurious rights,
mocking compassion.
Regardless of belief, all
suffer—and die all the same.

Winter

In these final weeks,
with travel and gatherings
restricted, the world
hollow and grieving the dead,
hope insubstantial as ash,

the holidays loom,
altered and inadequate:
No presents, no prayers
can offset the past twelve months'
irredeemable losses.

Even so, we wait,
damaged and so damned tired
of it all, aching
for whatever can begin
healing us in the new year.

THE PATCHWORK REVISITED

I am sometimes
the aging quilt,
slowly unfolded,
laid out, all in.

I am often
the gutted corner,
batting gone, unable
to keep warm.

I am always
the loose thread,
twisted and aimless,
awaiting the shears.

CALAMITY COMES CALLING

For Robert Lavett Smith

Last night I dreamed of Calamity.

I stand alone on hard, cracked earth
in the middle of Main Street, shackled by bitter heat,
pressed beneath a sepia sky blemished only
by a few listless buzzards and the cigarette burn
of the sun. The wind, its low wail rough and desperate,
scrapes over the town's blighted bones like a planchette
blindly spelling out its message of ruin. A litter of rats
squirms in the flare of a crumpled gramophone horn.
In the surrounding distance, locusts feed in a frenzy
of clicking mandibles, ferociously laying to waste
what little remains of living prairie.

I woke with aching joints
and a mouth dry as dust; later,
as I brushed, hair drifted to the floor
like twisted wisps of dead grass.

BREAK

Broken, I am fixed
between the past with its spilled
button-jar memories, and the future,
now written in a language
I don't recognize; caught
in the synaptic space between
thought and action, between
silent cold and a match-struck flame
that shouts its small, reckless presence.

That future is coming, though,
ready or not. I feel it reaching for me
the same way that unseen heat
reveals itself in seething shadows
tattooed by the winter sun
on a building's skin.

LOVE ONE SUNDAY MORNING

We are a fugue, and the sun
pours through the window
to listen.

LESSON

"Pain comes from the darkness
and we call it wisdom. It is pain."
—*Randall Jarrell*

Part 1: A Fragment of Summer

Together
decades ago: a warm afternoon
on Route 116, rolling past the simple splendor
of golden fields and Oreo cows,
clouds drowsing high above,
sweeps of sun flicking
through the eucalyptus.

Time yet for everything.

Part 2: How It Is

At first, the shock
is fresh and deceptive, like scalding:
so hot it feels cold, light as an insult.

At first.

Over time, though, grief settles heavy,
deeper and truer.
Longing becomes a freezing ache,
iron teeth that slowly grind bone
into dust so cold
it burns.

BATTLEGROUND

i.m. Michael James Lamp (1956–2013)

The opening skirmishes
took place in late autumn
when the enemy slid in
and hid in plain sight, disguised
as a little extra fatigue, perhaps;
an occasional prickle deep
under your breastbone, nudging
alongside chronic indigestion;
a stubborn January cold.

In a matter of weeks,
the invading armies grew
bolder, impostors spreading
corruption like rumors. The first whispers
aimed themselves at the base
of your esophagus and strafed it raw;
others thudded into your liver,
blasting it with tumors; multitudes ran
through miles of blood and intestine,
laying your system to ruin,
silent and swift.

By early February, your body rang
with alarms at last: yellow warnings
in your eyes and skin, pain's drumbeat
now audible. Only days later,
as night surrendered to dawn,
you choked on blood black as ink
fleeing your shredded throat
like some dark sea creature
spooling from your mouth
into a basin I held while dialing 9-1-1.

In the hospital—
among the ice chips, the tangle
of lines leading in and out,
the rampart of our clasped hands,
the white field—the final battle
began, all too soon and far too late.
And there, despite everything,
you drove fear into the ground
and fought to a draw:
Death didn't *take* you. You rose
instead to meet it and strode with it
from this world
unbowed.

LUCKY

You're so lucky to have a house,
I've been told, given the high price
of real estate in the San Francisco Bay Area.

Paid for with the life of my soul mate,
I think to myself, it's hardly a bargain;
sure, I still have the house—
but my home is gone.

TEMPORARY RETREAT

I enter the lavatory
of the hospital room
where you lie dying,
shutting the door behind me,
gratefully alone
for only these few moments.
Looking at the call lever
next to the toilet, I silently scoff—
as if yanking a string could summon
any sort of meaningful help—and then
my mouth stretches wide
open in a soundless scream
over and over; eyes, throat, fists,
and body clenched, shuddering
to relieve some of the terrible
pressure in my heart
before I return to your bedside
to hold your hand, trying to reassure
us both.

WARRIOR

i.m. Michael James Lamp (1956-2013)

You deserved a Viking funeral:
proud ship ablaze with glorious fire
in the sea's welcoming clasp; the wind fresh and wild,
howling a dirge as the smoke rose high;
alongside your body the fine bow and arrows
you carefully crafted, fitting weaponry
for your warrior soul.

Instead,
we hailed you farewell
in a claustrophobic hospital room;
we consigned your abandoned flesh and bones
to a cardboard vessel and the impassive retort
of a crematorium;
we placed your ashes by handfuls
on open land at the end of an archery range
without barrow or marker,
our whispered tributes lost
almost instantly to the restless air.

Yet, despite these failings,
we gently, reverently
laid our hands upon you
to warm you as you sank
by morphine's mercy
into dreamless final hours
adrift on your white cotton pyre,
until you slipped your earthly moorings
at last, transcendent;
and we now—as then—hold you
forever honored in the watery chambers
of our charred, ruined hearts.

YOUR REVISED LIFE

Summary of edits:

Heart broken
into smaller sections;
grief inserted where marked.

All other parts
given more weight;
pain added, especially
in later chapters;
"lover" replaced throughout
with "laptop."

Margins narrowed;
empty space increased.

Ending totally rewritten.

Read it.

Weep.

THANKSGIVING

Even in my dreams I know you're dead,
have always known it fully from the instant
I learned you were gone.

I've never since woken happy
believing you're still alive. For this
I'm thankful.

LIFE AFTER A DEATH

You exist
mostly by default.

After an initial burst
of desperate energy, you start to drift,
and things that seemed to matter, matter less
and less until they simply don't.
Classic sign of depression, you recognize,
but don't care. Of course.
You smile wryly at that
even as it annoys you to admit it.
And anyway, you can stop, regroup,
and get on with it anytime.
Any time at all.

But you don't (of course).
Something else always defeats you first:
the weather, the temperature, insomnia,
the fact that you have to work,
the fact that you don't have to work,
a cold, a fever, a headache, a hangnail. . .
and so it goes.

You feel increasingly
like a wooden jumble of limbs pulled
on the one hand by obligation
and basic creature needs;
on the other hand by loss and longing
and—worst of all—hope,
tenacity its most defining quality
and its cruelest.

One day, you notice
you no longer see yourself
in the hollow stranger you've become,
as little you as any corpse
is its former living self;
and you wonder, somewhat stunned,
when this happened—when,
and perhaps how, but not why. That much
you do know.

But then you begin to write.

You write about the sugar bowl.

Your gaze often rests
on the pale yellow sugar bowl—

lid lost long before you bought it
because you liked its shape, its elegant lines—
still useful, but no longer able to hold
and protect anything sweet
from being defiled.

You write about the dust.

Ah, that dust, persistent, insolent,
mocking you from all surfaces; and yet
you simply cannot find the energy
to clear it, or to care about clearing it,
or even to care about not caring
enough to clear it.
And so the dead dust stays,
settling on everything like sadness.

You write about the lightbulbs.

One by one,
almost all of your lights have burned out.
You bother keeping only two lamps
alive with working bulbs,
leaving the others with their shattered filaments

in mute darkness.
On bright days, brief trips outside—
to the porch for mail,
to the driveway to move trash bins—
make the cells in your eyes
tremble uneasily.

And then you really begin to write:
about death, yes, but also
about water, about fire,
about music and art;
about eggs and ships, and stones as talismans;
about people you once knew and loved;
about poetry itself.

You note with hesitant wonder that small joys
do still occur; you find you can even laugh.
Your blown heart shifts, and you realize
there's still fight in you,
at least for now.

Maybe today, you'll change a lightbulb.

MAYBE. . .

. . .it's the earth instead in reluctant thrall
to the moon; the ocean lies perfectly still,
and it's the sand that roils the water, the ground
that fidgets and bucks beneath it,
keeping it forever unsettled.

. . .notes strike the strings, making hammers jump
and keys pull at a pianist's fingers;
melodies soar down brass throats in a rush
to work the valves and fill the lungs of trumpeters;
air vibrates to lure a tune.

. . .I'm the one who died, who's now becalmed
on a motionless sea, anchored to memory,
listening endlessly to music played
by musicians long dead, while you remain in our house,
drifting to and fro, days, nights, year after year
through the silent rooms, speaking to me
as if I were really still there to answer.

Index of Titles

About the Author

Janet Wildung currently survives near San Francisco, where she enjoys creativity fueled by a random blend of insomnia, synesthesia, and chronically restless eclecticism. This is her first book of poems. She is not quitting her day job. Yet.

www.ingramcontent.com/pod-product-compliance
Lightning Source LLC
Chambersburg PA
CBHW020909090426
42736CB00008B/555